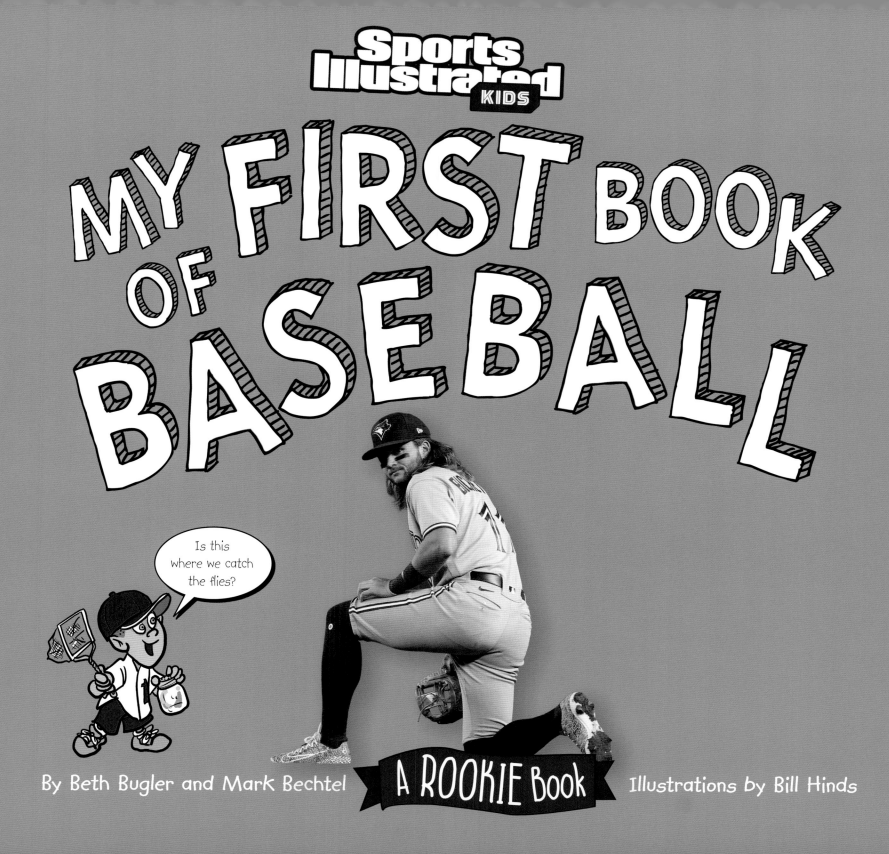

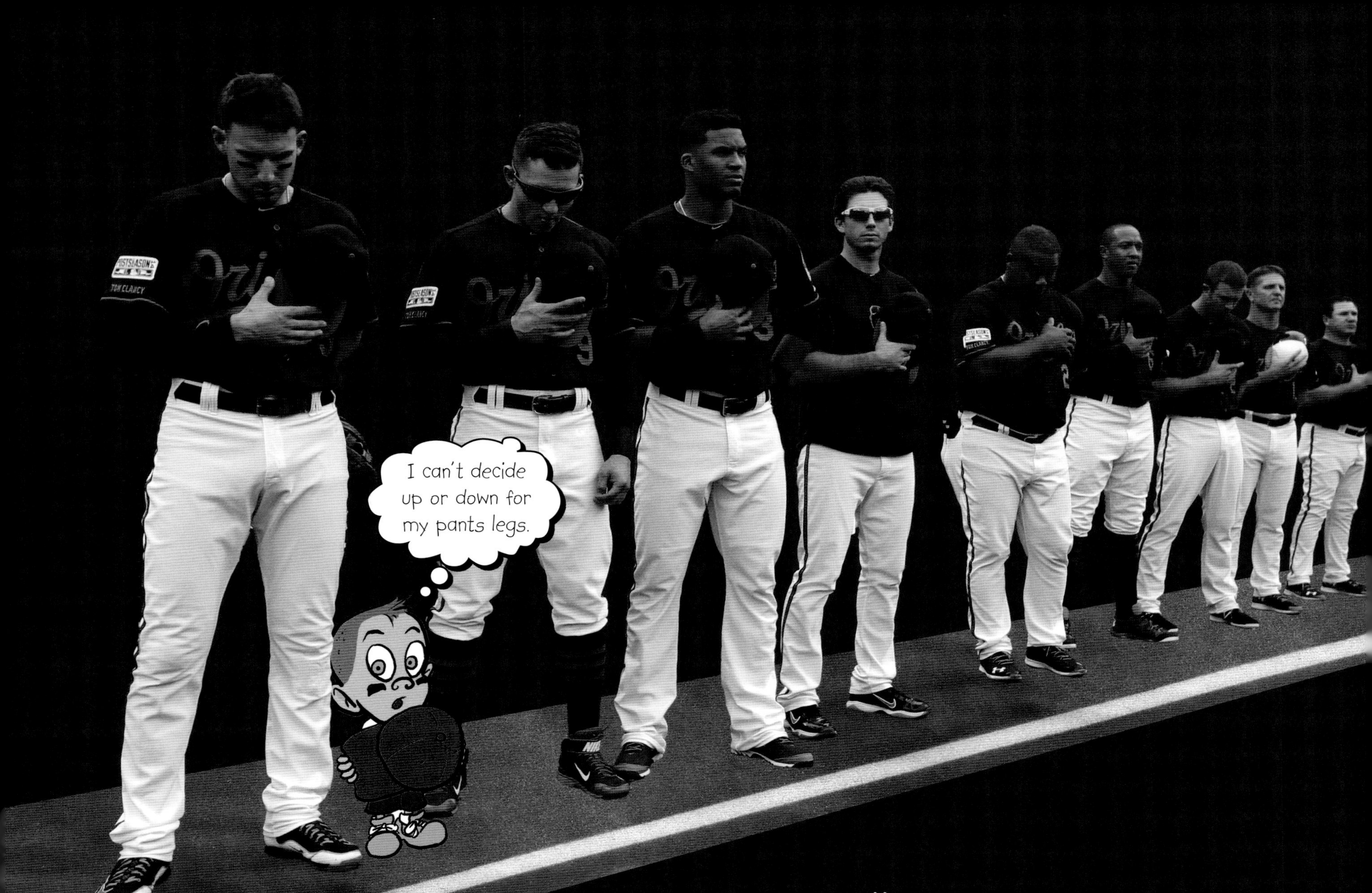

Baseball is a game between

TWO TEAMS.

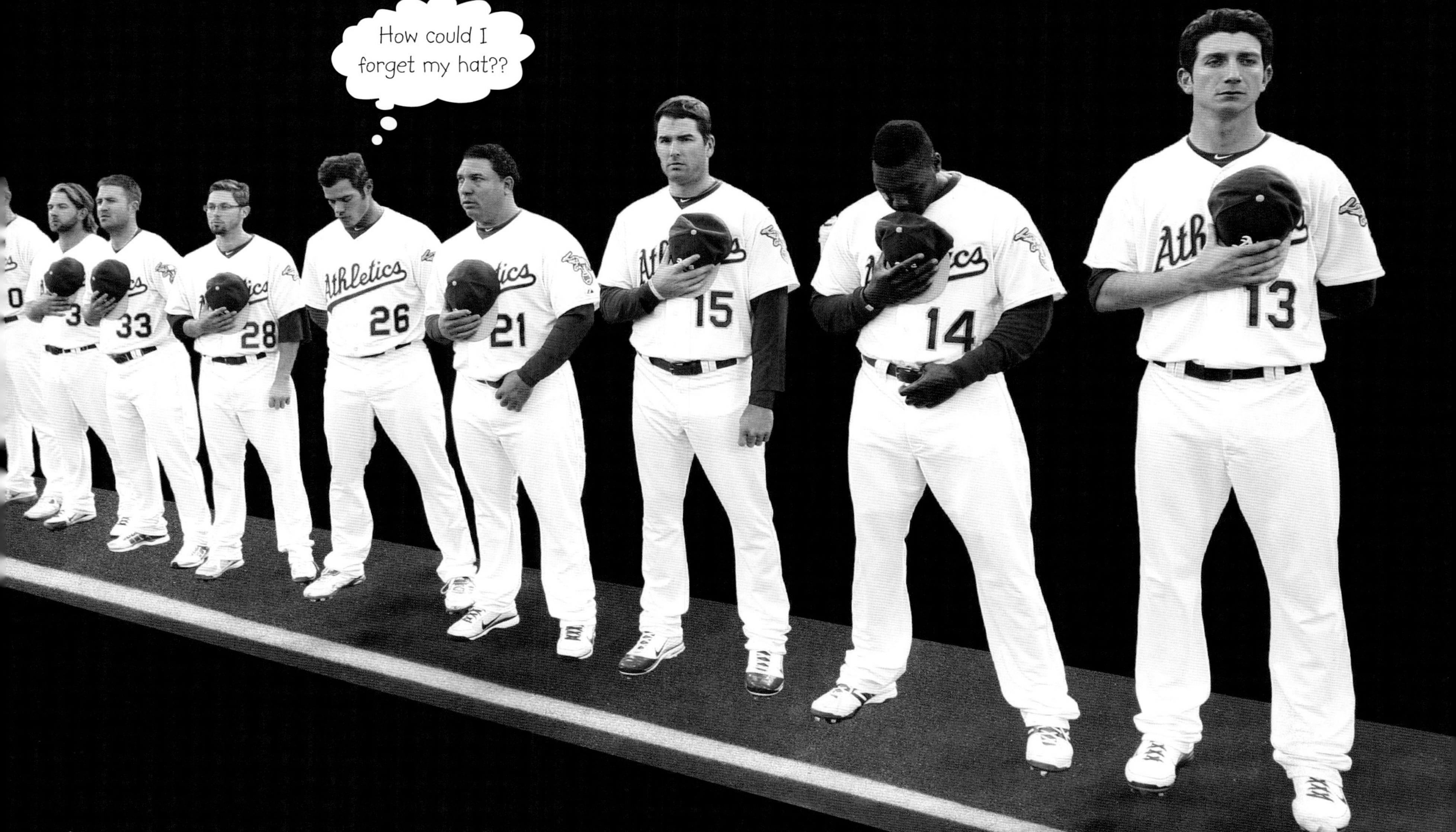

Each team is made up of

NINE PLAYERS.

Unlike most sports, baseball has no running clock. Instead, the game is played for nine

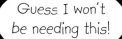

Guess I won't be needing this!

INNINGS.

Each inning has two parts:

TOP OF THE INNING	The visiting team is on offense and the home team plays defense.
BOTTOM OF THE INNING	The home team is on offense and the visiting team plays defense.

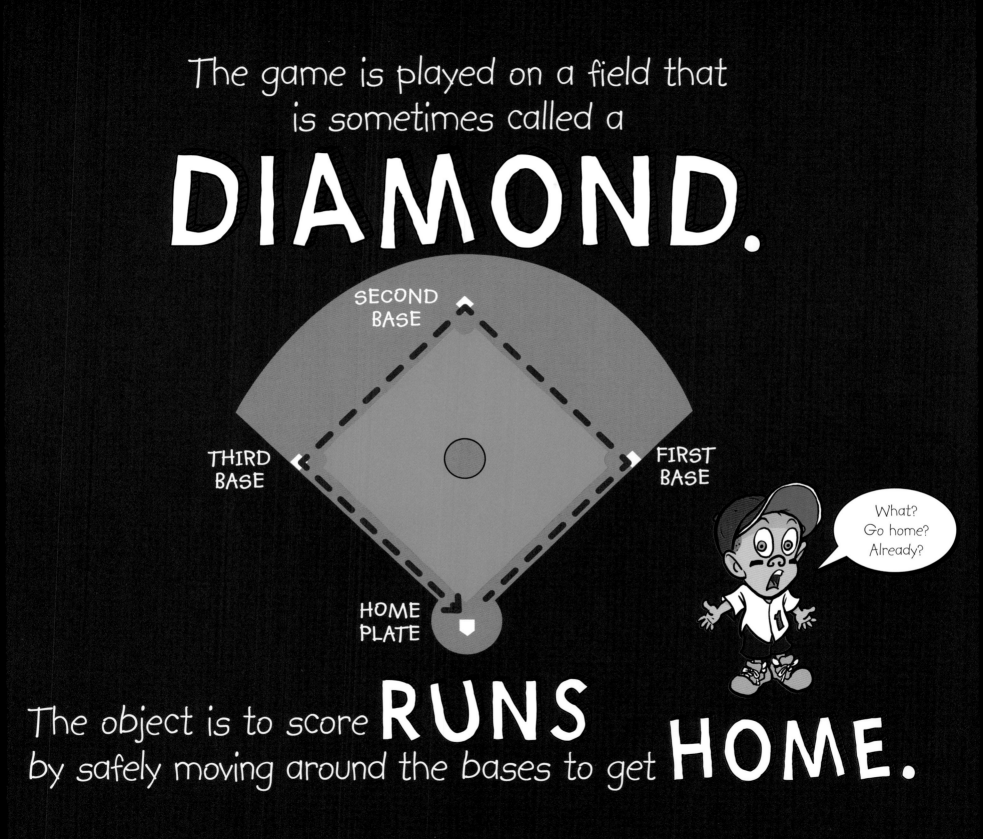

The guys with the bats are the

OFFENSE.

The players with the gloves are the

DEFENSE.

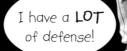

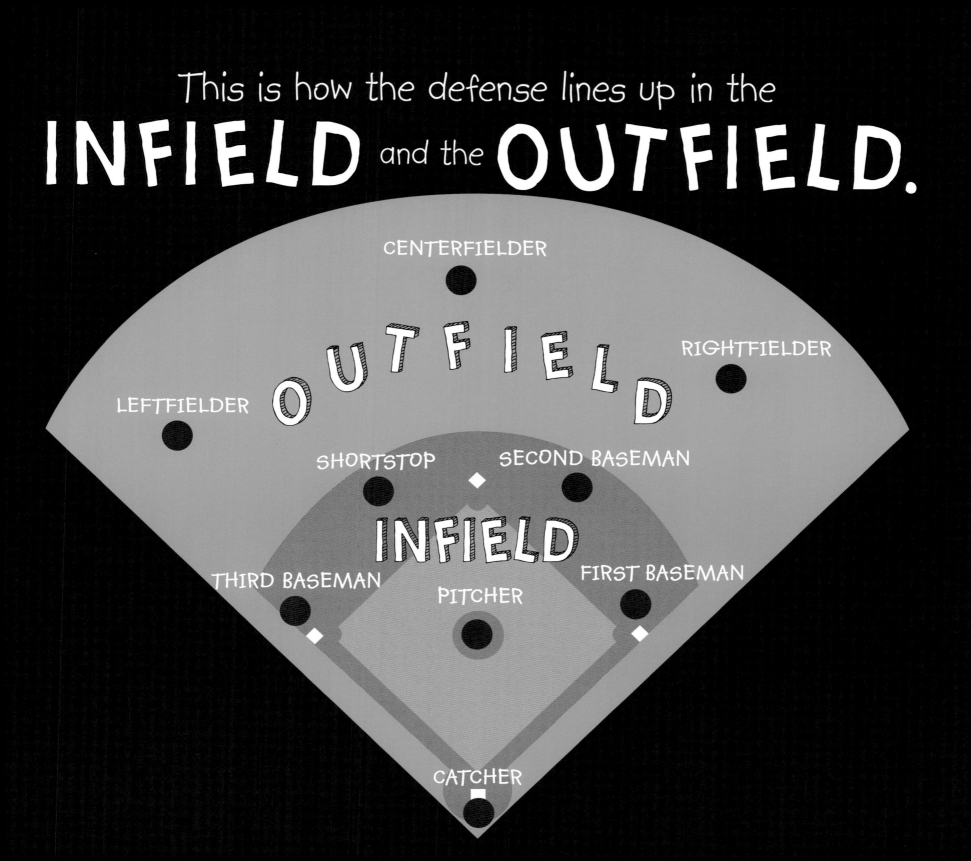

I know I usually hit third, but today I want to go first!

The first

BATTER

from the visiting team steps up to home plate.

Sixty feet, six inches away, the

VISITOR **0**

HOME **0**

The batter looks over at the third base coach.

They are each looking for a

SIGN

to tell them what to do.

And what are **YOU** looking at?

CABRERA
24

INNING 2

The pitcher throws the ball.

I'm heading to the outfield!

VISITOR 0
HOME 0

The batter
SWINGS,
and it's a . . .

FLY BALL!

The batter hits the ball high in the air. The defense tries to catch the ball before it hits the ground.

If you don't get it, I'm totally on it!

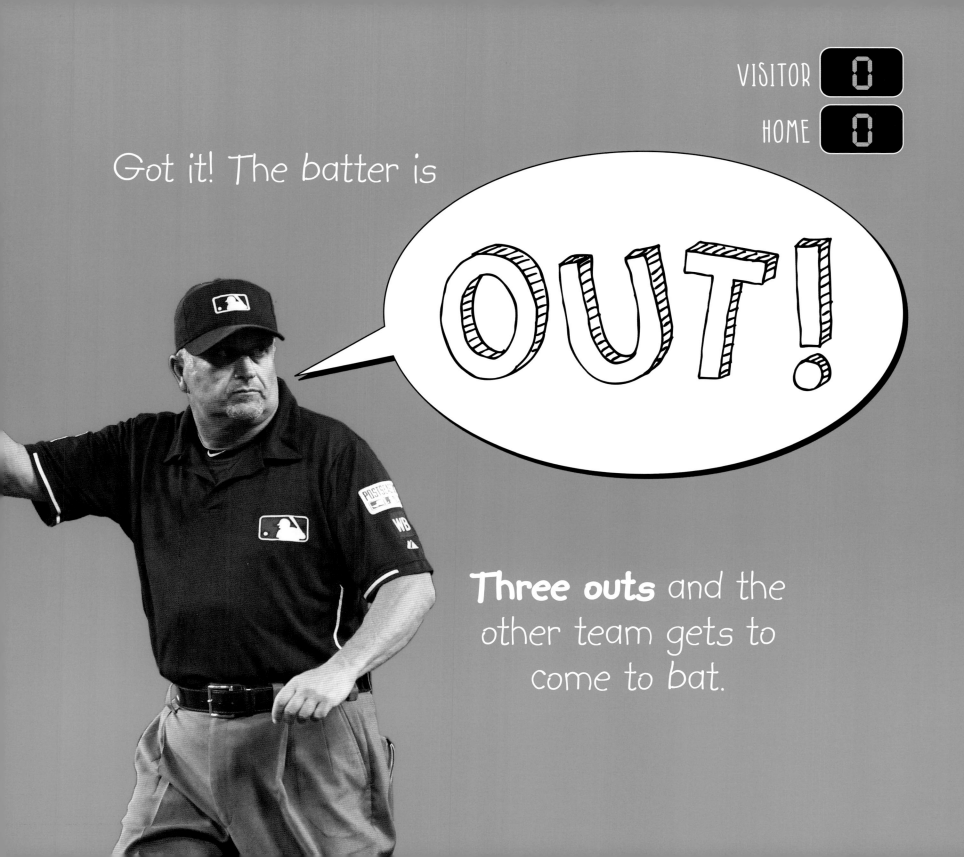

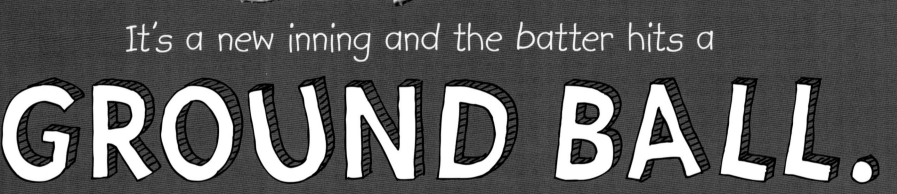

It's a new inning and the batter hits a

GROUND BALL.

The ball rolls toward a fielder, who tries to scoop it up and throw it to first base before the batter gets there.

INNING

3

The batter got there before the ball! He's

SAFE!

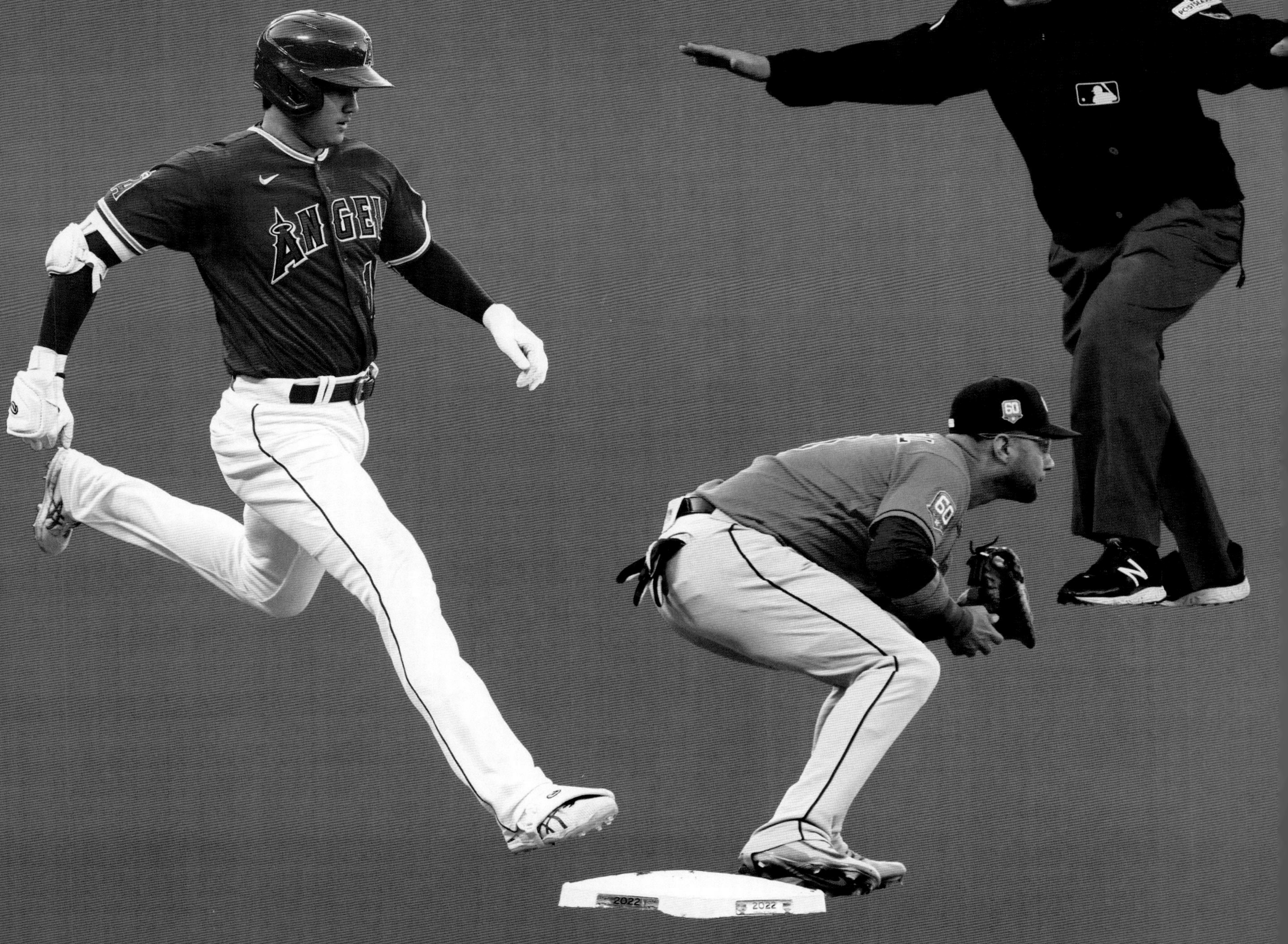

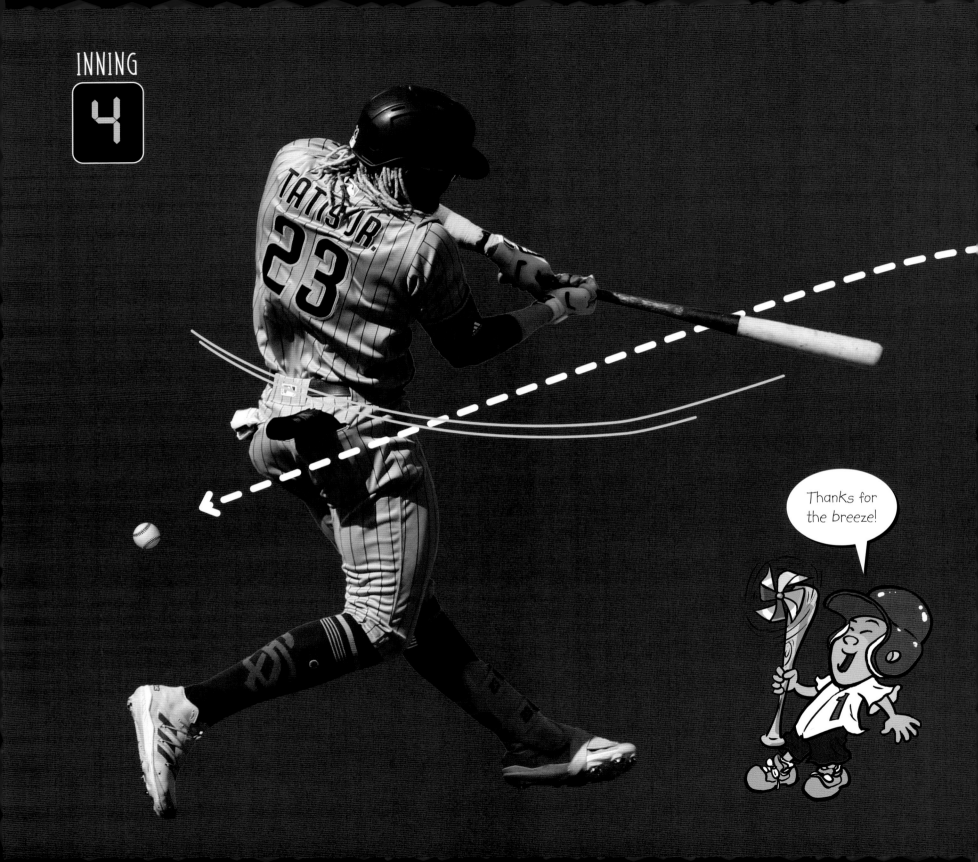

The pitcher throws the pitch.
The batter swings and misses.

STRIKE ONE!

Three strikes and you're out!

The pitcher tries to throw a ball that is hard to hit, but it must be in the

STRIKE ZONE.

That's the area over home plate between the batter's knees and chest.

If the hitter doesn't swing at a pitch that's over the plate, it's a strike.

Good luck hitting my strike zone!

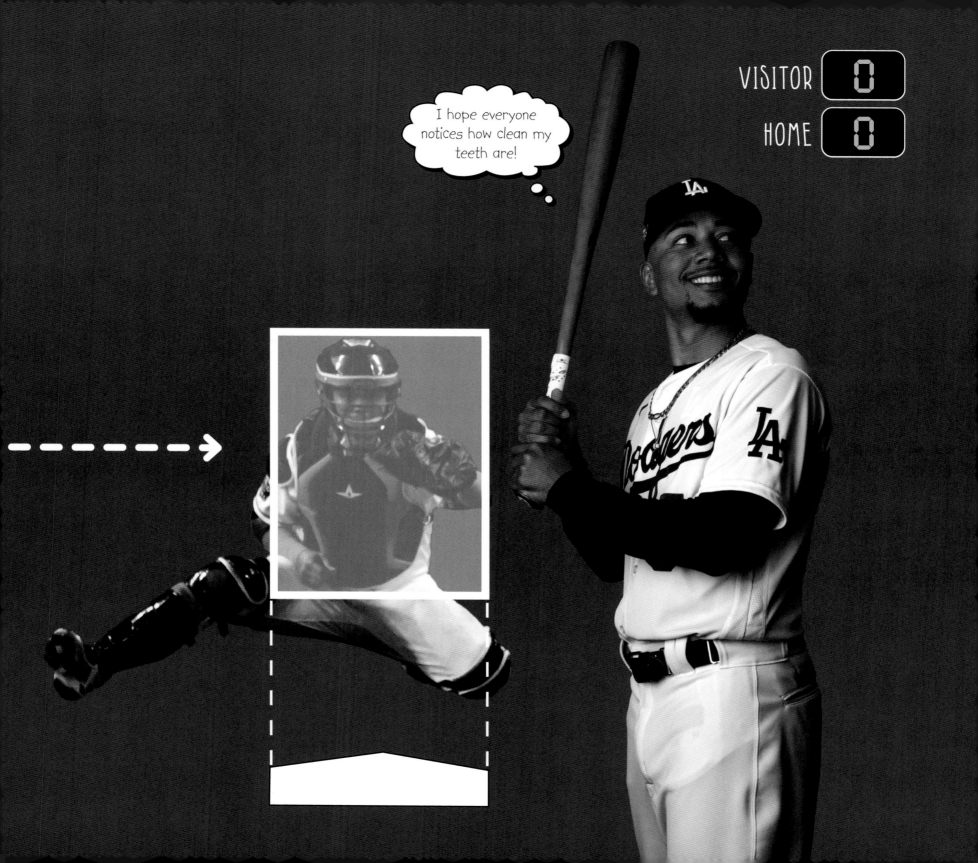

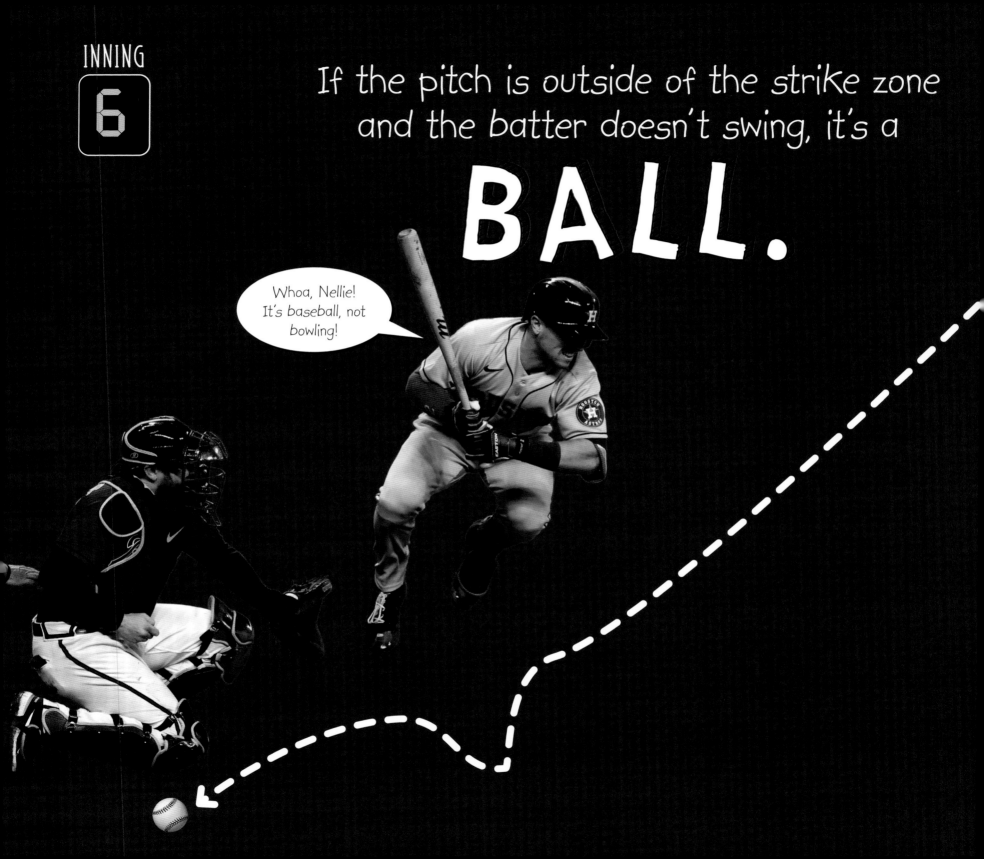

Four balls is a

WALK,

and the batter gets to go to first base.

Geez, slow down! It's called a walk, not a jog!

This hitter CRUSHES

the ball, and everyone is off! The batter runs to first, the runner on first takes off for second, and the runner on second heads for third!

The defense tries to get the ball back to the infield as fast as it can.

VISITOR 0

HOME 0

You go there next.

Yay! The runner from second base makes it past third and crosses home plate. His team scores a

RUN!

. . . the runner from first base is trying to make it all the way to third. But the defense gets the ball to the third baseman, who

TAGS

the runner before he gets to the base.
He's out!

So . . . tag, you're not "it," you're "out!"

That's the end of the top of the seventh inning.
Since we've been at it for so long, it's time for the . . .

7TH INNING STRETCH

Stand up. Shake it out.
Sing "Take Me Out to the Ball Game,"
and take care of your business.

We're done stretching and ready to get back to the action. He swings and belts the ball . . .

SOTO
22

The score is tied. The batter takes a big swing, but the ball doesn't go onto the field. It's a

FOUL BALL

because it's outside the foul lines.

MINE!

FOUL LINE

That counts as a **strike** — and the fan in the stands who caught the ball gets to keep it!

Now we're in the bottom of the ninth, and the game is still tied. The offense has a runner on every base.

Pants are feeling a bit tight. Too many nachos?

The **BASES** are **LOADED.**

INNING 9

The defense really needs an out. A run here means the home team will win the game. So the manager comes to the mound to talk strategy.

I was three minutes away from a really good nap.

The manager decides that his pitcher is getting too tired, so he brings in a fresh, rested pitcher from the

BULLPEN.

Wait, you were resting and not roping steer back there?

This is a huge moment. Can he get the big out?

No! The batter smacks the ball over the fence. **HOME RUN!** He scores, and the other three runners do, too. It's a

GRAND

GAME OVER!

It's time to celebrate!

Copyright © 2023 ABG-SI LLC. Used under license. Sports Illustrated Kids™ is a trademark of ABG-SI LLC.

No part of this publication may be reproduced, stored in a retrieval system, or transmitted in any form by any means, electronic, mechanical, photocopying, or otherwise, without the prior written permission of the publisher, Triumph Books LLC, 814 North Franklin Street, Chicago, Illinois 60610.

Library of Congress Cataloging-in-Publication Data available upon request.

Printed in China
ISBN 978-1-63727-502-3

This book is available in quantity at special discounts for your group or organization. For further information, contact:
    Triumph Books LLC
    814 North Franklin Street
    Chicago, Illinois 60610
    (312) 337-0747
    www.triumphbooks.com